Communications Plan for the Great Lakes Inventory and Monitoring Network (2010-2014)

Natural Resource Report NPS/GLKN/NRR—2009/157

I0415814

Ted Gostomski
National Park Service
Great Lakes Inventory and Monitoring Program
2800 Lakeshore Drive East, Suite D
Ashland, Wisconsin 54806

October 2009

U.S. Department of the Interior
National Park Service
Natural Resource Program Center
Fort Collins, Colorado

The National Park Service, Natural Resource Program Center publishes a range of reports that address natural resource topics of interest and applicability to a broad audience in the National Park Service and others in natural resource management, including scientists, conservation and environmental constituencies, and the public.

The Natural Resource Report Series is used to disseminate high-priority, current natural resource management information with managerial application. The series targets a general, diverse audience, and may contain NPS policy considerations or address sensitive issues of management applicability.

All manuscripts in the series receive the appropriate level of peer review to ensure that the information is scientifically credible, technically accurate, appropriately written for the intended audience, and designed and published in a professional manner. This report received informal peer review by subject-matter experts who were not directly involved in the collection, analysis, or reporting of the data.

Views, statements, findings, conclusions, recommendations, and data in this report are those of the author(s) and do not necessarily reflect views and policies of the National Park Service, U.S. Department of the Interior. Mention of trade names or commercial products does not constitute endorsement or recommendation for use by the National Park Service.

This report is available from the Great Lakes Inventory and Monitoring Program website (http://science.nature.nps.gov/im/units/GLKN/reportpubs.cfm) and the Natural Resource Publications Management website (http://www.nature.nps.gov/publications/NRPM).

Please cite this publication as:

Gostomski, T. 2009. Communications plan for the Great Lakes Inventory and Monitoring Network (2010-2014). Natural Resource Report NPS/GLKN/NRR—2009/157. National Park Service, Fort Collins, Colorado.

NPS 999/100544, October 2009

Table of Contents

Figures

Tables

Appendices

Abstract

The Great Lakes Inventory and Monitoring Program has a diverse set of audiences to whom we must direct very specific, tailored information about who we are, what we do, and why we do it. Communication is not the end product of our monitoring programs, but it is an essential and ongoing process of keeping park staff informed about every facet of our operation, from who will be working in what parks and when, to what we are learning from our monitoring programs and how what we learn can be used to inform park management decisions.

This Communications Plan outlines the Great Lakes Inventory and Monitoring Program's communication goals for the next five years. It identifies our target audiences, and it lays out our objectives and the strategies we will use to achieve those objectives. This plan also articulates our main messages, identifies some of the products and media we will use, outlines the procedures we will use to evaluate the effectiveness of those products, and presents an annual calendar of when products must be distributed so that we are providing the best information and tools in a timely manner to the Network parks we serve, our partners, and the public.

1. Background and Justification

The National Park Service Organic Act of 1916 articulates the agency's mission to conserve scenery, natural and historic objects, and wildlife found in the national parks for the enjoyment of current and future generations. Interpreters and law enforcement rangers have worked the frontline of this mission, helping park visitors to understand the significance of natural and historic features and the importance of protecting them. However, attempts to provide more in-depth scientific information to managers and subsequently to interpreters have not always been met with enthusiasm, and have even been met with outright disdain (see Sellars 1997). Several attempts to improve the relationship between science and management yielded varying degrees of success until the National Parks Omnibus Management Act of 1998 and the Natural Resource Challenge (1999) mandated a shift to management decision-making based on the scientific knowledge. Along with management's increased emphasis on scientific knowledge came a stated intent to share information widely with all concerned audiences.

> *Once this* [inventory and monitoring] *information is in our hands, we must share it widely, so that child and adult, amateur and professional can benefit from the knowledge uncovered in these places. The information contained in the parks should help the surrounding communities, both regional and global, in making choices about their future. ...To unlock this information, we need to revitalize and expand our natural resource programs, strengthen partnerships with the scientific community, and* **share knowledge with educational institutions and the public** (NPS 1999: p. 3; emphasis added).

This intent basically continues the National Park Service's long-standing interpretive duty, but it also suggests a stronger relationship between interpreters and park scientists and resource managers so that "the expanding body of knowledge" gleaned from inventory and monitoring of natural resources is "professionally managed [and] widely disseminated to the public" (NPS 1999: p. 9).

Why would we do this? Why would scientists and resource managers become, in a sense, interpreters and educators? Because "protection of park resources requires a knowledgeable public" (NPS 1999: p. 11), and, as noted by Soukup (2007), "when combined with an effective education program, monitoring results can contribute not only to park issues, but also to larger quality-of-life issues that affect surrounding communities and can contribute significantly to the environmental health of the nation."

The source of scientific knowledge on which management would rely, in addition to existing resource management programs within individual parks, was established through the Natural Resource Challenge (NPS 1999). Part of "the Challenge," a Service-wide effort to bolster science and resource management in the parks, was the development of a national Inventory and Monitoring Program that works with individual parks to develop and execute long-term monitoring of the parks' most critical natural resources. Thirty-two inventory and monitoring networks were established, and 270 national park units were included in these networks that formed around common geography and resource management issues. In the Great Lakes region, nine parks in four states comprise the Great Lakes Inventory and Monitoring Network (GLKN).

Who, What, and Why: The Mission of the Great Lakes Inventory and Monitoring Program

The **purpose** of the National Park Service's Inventory and Monitoring (I&M) program is to identify and monitor key elements of park ecosystems ("Vital Signs") to help detect ecological problems that need further research or management action. Specifically, Service-wide **goals** for Vital Signs monitoring, as stated by Fancy (2004), are to:

1. Determine the status and trends of selected indicators of park ecosystem conditions so that managers can make better-informed decisions and work more effectively with other agencies and individuals for the benefit of park resources.
2. Provide early warning of abnormal conditions and impairment of selected resources to promote effective mitigation and reduce management costs.
3. Provide data to better understand the dynamic nature and condition of park ecosystems and to provide reference points for comparisons with other altered environments.
4. Provide data to meet certain legal and congressional mandates related to natural resource protection and visitor enjoyment.
5. Provide a means of measuring progress towards achieving performance goals that are mandated by Government Performance Results Act (GPRA).

The Great Lakes Network adopted these Service-wide goals and further defined the **intentions and limitations** of the Network's program with the following provisions (Route and Elias 2007, emphasis added):

1. The majority of the Network's funding and efforts will be directed at *monitoring trends in resource themes or issues that are common across Network parks and that individual parks would find difficult to accomplish due to high cost, magnitude of scale, or lack of expertise*. This commonality across parks and monitoring themes will <u>increase staff efficiency and cost-effectiveness, promote sharing of data, and allow comparison of trends across the Network</u>.
2. In cases where Vital Signs are already being monitored by one or more parks, and the Network assumes the cost of monitoring, the park(s) agree(s) to re-allocate park-based funds and staff to other natural resource efforts in that park. Parks will continue to monitor various resources not monitored by the Network, conduct short-term assessments and field studies, and facilitate research.
3. The Network's monitoring program will be <u>designed with quality of information in mind, not the number of issues addressed</u>. The *objective is to provide high quality data on a core set of resource indicators*. Additional research and park-based monitoring can expand from this core set of indicators.
4. The Network will strive for multiple lines of evidence to document significant changes in resource status. Further, we expect that trends in Vital Signs will provide a basis for developing and testing hypotheses for cause-and-effect research. It is the shared responsibility of the Network, each individual park, the Great Lakes Research and Education Center, and our science partners to uncover important trends in Vital Signs and seek funding to conduct research on the causes and effects of such trends.

5. The Network monitoring program will *strive for consistency in long-term data collection* yet allow for flexibility to alter or remove indicators that are not meeting objectives.

2. Communicating the Science of Monitoring

The Information Iceberg

Understandable and useful information is developed from the data we collect, but data alone are not intuitive to the public or even to other National Park Service employees. Indeed, they can be dangerous if taken and used out of context. The raw data must be organized and analyzed, the statistics and findings resulting from the analyses put into technical reports and peer-reviewed papers, and the technical reports and papers used to develop messages and materials directed at a non-technical audience.

The process through which raw data become simple, clear, useful messages is illustrated by the "information iceberg" (Figure 1). The amount of information and its accompanying data becomes more finely-tuned and clearer as it moves up the iceberg. Each layer has its own audience, and even raw data is something that can be communicated without any interpretation, but only if the audience to which it is being transmitted is capable of understanding it. In other words, the audience for a particular message determines the level of information that will be communicated. This is true for both external (public) and internal (park) audiences. This layered approach is similar to an iceberg in that most public audiences will only see the "tip" and not the data and other information that form the foundation or base of the iceberg.

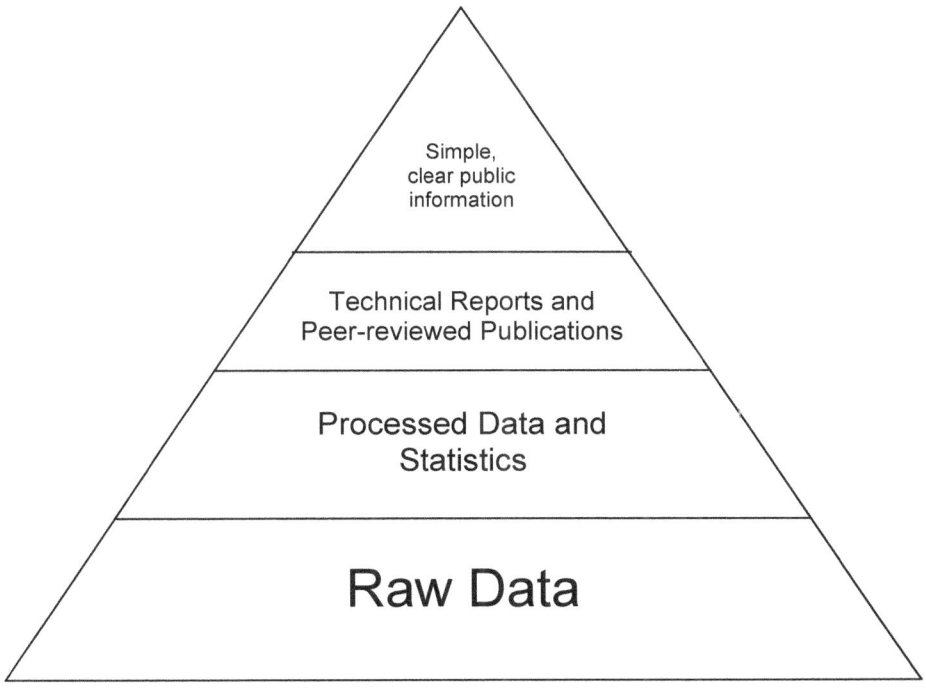

Figure 1. The information iceberg. Based on Fancy (2008).

Audiences

Our audiences are internal and external to the National Park Service, and they have varying degrees of scientific knowledge. They also have varying commitments to us and the success of our program. Therefore, products and media we use to disseminate information must always keep in mind who the audience is so that we engage to the fullest their interest in us and our success.

Fancy et al. (2009) stated that the primary audience and users of the data gathered through I&M programs are managers, planners, natural resource specialists, interpreters, and scientists at the local park level. They also said that monitoring results can be provided to the general public in partnership with other NPS programs and park interpreters. This sets a clear communication hierarchy for us to follow: we serve the parks and the parks serve the public. However, we can help inform park staff so that their presentations to the public regarding natural resource issues include some of the most up-to-date information that is coming out of our monitoring programs.

Based on the above guidelines, our audiences (in priority order) are:

1. Park Staff
    a. Resource managers
    b. Superintendents
    c. Interpreters
    d. Law enforcement rangers
    e. Maintenance and other field staff
    f. Administrative support staff

2. Partners
    a. Collaborators/contractors (those who are assisting with monitoring or who are contracted to undertake an entire program)
    b. Agencies (federal and state)
    c. Tribal entities (especially those with adjoining property boundaries)
    d. Adjacent landowners
    e. Non-government organizations (includes universities and other academia)

3. Peers – the scientific community both within and outside the National Park Service.

4. The Public
    a. The park visitors that Network staff come into contact with during the course of our work.
    b. The park visitors that park interpreters will reach using information and tools we provide.

Key Messages

Key messages, or "talking points," about the mission and purpose of the Great Lakes Inventory and Monitoring Program can be inferred from the purpose and goals of the Service-wide I&M program (Fancy 2004) and from the intentions and limitations of the Great Lakes Network (Route and Elias 2007), both of which are summarized on page 2 of this plan. Based on those statements, key messages that should be communicated to the parks and the public are as follows:

1. The Great Lakes Inventory and Monitoring Program establishes and conducts long-term monitoring programs that address natural resource issues common to all nine parks in the Great Lakes Network.

2. Park managers selected the natural resource issues ("Vital Signs") to be monitored based on individual park priorities and then on inter-park similarities. Consequently, the Great Lakes I&M Program serves (rather than oversees) the nine parks of the Great Lakes Network.

3. Network staff (rather than park staff) coordinate and manage these monitoring programs because long-term monitoring and inter-park (regional) analyses and summaries are often something that individual parks do not have the time, staff, or money to do. Thus, park staff are free to pursue more park-specific management issues.

4. The Great Lakes I&M Program staff are not an additional layer of resource management in the parks. Rather, they are field staff and scientists who provide data and information so that park managers can make more informed decisions regarding the management of the lands in their care.

5. Whereas the individual parks are ultimately focused on their park-specific management issues, Network staff are charged with putting parks in a regional context by interpreting the data from a regional perspective.

3. Communication Types

This section, adapted from Beever and Sanders (2007), summarizes all the reporting and communications products identified in the Great Lakes Network's long-term monitoring plan, including prescribed due dates for some materials. To facilitate a clearer picture of the Network's outreach responsibilities and targets, the information is condensed into a bulleted format, and audiences and affected staff (who is responsible for producing the item) have been added. Using this information, a Great Lakes Network communications calendar was created (Appendix A), which distills even further the products and their respective due dates into a format that Network staff can use for planning and prioritizing. Some of these communication media will be developed and implemented in conjunction with staff at the Great Lakes Research and Education Center.

Written Media

Annual Data Summary Reports
- Affected Staff – Program Managers, collaborating partners/contractors, Science Writer.
- Purpose – To document our efforts, provide summary data, and convey the major findings of the previous field season without detailed interpretation or discussion. These are short, concise presentations of the year's field work.
- Style – Technical, following Natural Resource Data Summary (NRDS) report format provided by Natural Resource Program Center's national report series. Reports in the national series are subjected to a peer-review process, completion of which is the responsibility of the primary author.
- Audience – Primary audience is the park staff. Collaborators and partners may also receive these reports or be able to access them through the Network website.
- Timeline – Produced annually for each Vital Sign monitored during the previous year.
  - ❖ Drafts of annual summary reports will be <u>completed by January 15</u> for internal review.
  - ❖ The final reports will be provided to parks <u>on March 1</u> of the year following the monitoring.

Analysis and Synthesis Reports
- Affected Staff – Program Managers, collaborating partners/contractors, Science Writer.
- Purpose – Detailed reports in which a minimum of three years of data are analyzed and synthesized.
- Style – Written in the Natural Resource Technical Report (NRTR) format for inclusion in that series. The format is similar to a scientific journal article (abstract, introduction, methods, results, discussion, literature cited) and contains in-depth analyses and interpretation as outlined in the protocol. Reports in the national series are subjected to a peer-review process, completion of which is the responsibility of the primary author.
- Audience – Target audience of the analysis and synthesis reports will be the parks, the Network, both regional and Service-wide I&M, and the broader scientific community.
- Timeline – Produced on a periodic basis, but at least every 10 years (see individual protocols for detailed schedules). Frequency depends on the given Vital Sign (e.g., on the re-visit strategy and frequency).
  - ❖ Drafts will be <u>completed by January 31</u> of the appointed year.

❖ The final reports will be provided to parks <u>on April 1</u> of the year following the monitoring.

Scientific Journal Articles
- Affected Staff – Program Managers, Science Writer, Network Coordinator.
- Purpose – Reach the scientific community in a way that internal NPS reports cannot; promote collaborative investigation by members of the scientific community, either independently or in cooperation with the Network; and foster a greater understanding of ecosystem components and processes. These publications also substantiate our work and findings through exposure in the peer-reviewed literature.
- Style – Technical. Specific style/format will depend on target publication. Each publication must be reviewed by the Network Coordinator prior to submission. If warranted, the Coordinator will facilitate review by park, regional, or national personnel.
- Audience – The scientific community beyond the National Park Service.
- Timeline – Reviewers of analysis and syntheses reports will be asked to recommend whether publication is warranted and suggest appropriate journals. The [Science Writer] and Network Coordinator will track these recommendations and encourage and provide work time respectively.

Annual Administrative Report
- Affected Staff – Network Coordinator, Administrative Assistant, Program Managers.
- Purpose – Details the accomplishments of the previous fiscal year, presents the objectives for the following fiscal year, and accounts for Network spending.
- Style – Inclusive yet briefly highlight key findings in a clear and concise manner that is understandable to those without a scientific background.
- Audience – The Network Board of Directors and Technical Committee, and the Service-wide I&M Program. The Board of Directors and Technical Committee use this report to gauge the accomplishments of the program, while the Service-wide I&M Program uses it to develop a national report on NPS inventory and monitoring efforts, which is presented to the U.S. Congress.
- Timeline – Produced every November.
  ❖ Drafts of the report are submitted to the regional I&M Coordinator and the Network Board of Directors for review and approval <u>in late October</u> each year.
  ❖ The final reports will be provided to the Service-wide I&M Program <u>in November</u>.

Resource Briefs
- Affected Staff – Science Writer, Program Managers, Network Coordinator.
- Purpose – A condensed distillation of the important findings for each monitoring program (taken from the annual reports). These provide bullet-point information about and preliminary findings from current monitoring in each park.
- Style – Non-technical, and amply illustrated with photos, figures, and maps.
- Audience – Park superintendents and other non-resource management staff.
- Timeline – Annually
  ❖ Drafts will be completed <u>by February 15</u>.
  ❖ Final versions will be provided to parks <u>on April 1</u>.

GLKN Newsletter
- Affected Staff – Science Writer, Program Managers, Network Coordinator.
- Purpose – Provide a means of regular communication between Network Office and Parks.
- Style – Short articles about monitoring programs and preliminary findings; photo-rich; calendar of "events." File can be printed and mailed, and it will be posted on GLKN public website.
- Audience – Park staff, visitors to GLKN website, collaborators, and contractors. A mailing list will be maintained, and anyone can request to be included on it.
- Timeline – Twice a year, one in April (preview of field season) and the second in October (summary of season).

Brochure
- Affected Staff – Science Writer.
- Purpose – Provide basic information about the Great Lakes I&M Program and what we do.
- Style – Non-technical.
- Audience – Everyone.
- Timeline – Brochure was updated in 2007/2008. Future updates will occur as needed.

Articles in Park Newsletters
- Affected Staff – Science Writer, Program Managers.
- Purpose – Provide a means of regular communication between the Network Office and park visitors.
- Style – Non-technical articles about monitoring in the park.
- Audience – Park visitors.
- Timeline – Will follow production timeline set by parks.

Press Releases
- Affected Staff – Science Writer, Program Managers, Network Coordinator.
- Purpose – Describe the mission of the I&M Program and provide information about current monitoring specific to the park(s) in the targeted area. May be used to specifically "advertise" upcoming monitoring in a particular park, in which case the Science Writer will coordinate efforts with that park's public relations staff and/or superintendent.
- Style – Non-technical, photo-rich.
- Audience – Communities around Network parks.
- Timeline – When possible/as needed.

Magazine Articles
- Affected Staff – Science Writer, Program Managers, Network Coordinator.
- Purpose – Describe the mission of the I&M Program and provide information about current monitoring specific to the park(s) in the targeted area. May be used to specifically "advertise" upcoming monitoring in a particular park.
- Style – Non-technical, photo-rich.
- Audience – Communities around Network parks and the Great Lakes region.
- Timeline – When possible or by request.

GLKN Poster
- Affected Staff – Science Writer.
- Purpose – Provide eye-catching, very basic advertising for the Great Lakes I&M Program. May also describe the mission of the Service-wide I&M Program.
- Style – One or two versions with scenic photos of Network parks, the GLKN name and names of each Network park. May also include non-technical, written information on the back describing the mission of the I&M Program.
- Audience – Non-resource management park staff, visiting public at the parks, non-visiting public (posters could be made available in off-site visitor centers and Department of Transportation/Tourism welcome centers).
- Timeline – One-time production with re-printing as necessary. Could be updated in the future.

Presentations

Talking Points
- Affected Staff – All.
- Purpose – Develop and provide consistent message about individual monitoring programs, the overall Great Lakes Network program, or even the Service-wide I&M Program.
- Style – Simple, brief, (primarily) non-technical statements. Technical points may also be developed for discussions with science-oriented publics.
- Audience – Technical staff are the primary audience, while the secondary audience is usually non-resource management park staff, the visiting public at the parks, and sometimes the media. Individual programs may need talking points to hand out to field staff and contractors (primary audience) to ensure they have a common message for park staff, public, and media (secondary audience) they meet in the field.
- Timeline – As needed.

Annual Technical Committee Meeting
- Affected Staff – Network Coordinator, Program Managers.
- Purpose – Communicate to and invite comments from the Network Technical Committee on overall progress of the Network's programs. Present findings from previous year's monitoring and discuss plans for upcoming field season.
- Style – A concise synopsis of monitoring results as well as management considerations.
- Audience – Park resource management and interpretive staff.
- Timeline – Annually in March.

Seasonal Park Staff Orientation
- Affected Staff – Science Writer, Program Managers (possibly).
- Purpose – To interact with seasonal staff at Network parks and inform them about the I&M program and activities specific to the park for that summer. Also provides information to seasonal Interpretative staff to use in their own public programs throughout the summer.
- Style – Non-technical presentation using various media.

- Audience – Seasonal park staff and seasonal GLKN staff.
- Timeline – By request, though parks will be solicited for interest. Late May to early June.

Conferences
- Affected Staff – Program Managers.
- Purpose – To reach the broader scientific community, as well as land managers and conservation practitioners.
- Style – Standard scientific presentation using various media.
- Audience – Scientific community and others at regional and national scientific conferences.
- Timeline – When possible.
  - ❖ Potential conferences include those sponsored by the Ecological Society of America, Society for Conservation Biology, The Wildlife Society, International Association for Landscape Ecology, Natural Areas Association, and the George Wright Society. At a more local scale, the Western Great Lakes Research Conference and the St. Croix Research Rendezvous.

Park Lecture Series
- Affected Staff – Science Writer, Program Managers, collaborating partners/contractors.
- Purpose – To interact with the visiting public and staff at each of the Network parks and inform them about the I&M Program and activities specific to the park.
- Style – Non-technical presentation using various media.
- Audience – Visiting public at Network parks, park staff.
- Timeline – By request, though parks will be solicited for interest. These will given primarily during summer (June-August) when Program Managers are working in the parks, but possibly at other times of year.

General Public Presentations
- Affected Staff – Science Writer, Program Managers.
- Purpose – To interact with the public in the Great Lakes region and provide information about the I&M program, up-to-date results of monitoring programs, and activities specific to a given park depending on location.
- Style – Non-technical presentation using various media.
- Audience – Regional public, interest groups/organizations (e.g., local Audubon).
- Timeline – By request.

Traveling Display
- Affected Staff – Science Writer.
- Purpose – To provide a stand-alone information booth for the public to learn about the I&M program and activities specific to a given park depending on location. Can also be a booth with staff present to answer questions at park events (e.g., BioBlitz).
- Style – Non-technical presentation using primarily printed media but also interactive when staff are on hand.
- Audience – Regional public through park events or placement in visitor centers.
- Timeline – By request, but parks will be solicited for interest.

Electronic Media

"News for Parks" List-service
- Affected Staff – Science Writer.
- Purpose – Provide Network and park staff with a summary of current news through the dissemination of occasional Emails. Items will be relevant to park management, the region, or other general interests.
- Style – List of headlines, a brief summary (usually the opening paragraph), citation of the source, and a link to the full article.
- Audience – Network staff and park resource managers, interpreters, superintendents, and others who express an interest in receiving the occasional updates.
- Timeline – Approximately once a week, depending on "news load."

Radio/TV Spots
- Affected Staff – Science Writer, Program Managers, Network Coordinator.
- Purpose – Describe the mission of the I&M Program and provide information about current monitoring in each park.
- Style – Interview, non-technical.
- Audience – Policy makers, educators, and the general public.
- Timeline – When possible, but only after one-to-two years of monitoring.

Audio/Video Podcasts
- Affected Staff – Science Writer, Program Managers, Data Manager.
- Purpose – Provide short audio and video clips on our website that highlight field work being done by Network staff and partners and why it is important for the future of the Great Lakes national parks.
- Style – Documentary, interview, non-technical.
- Audience – Non-visiting public.
- Timeline – When possible.

Internet/Intranet
The Network's public website http://science.nature.nps.gov/im/units/glkn/ is the primary means of communicating information about our activities and findings. We have developed the website so that it is informative both to park staff and our partners and to individuals outside of the National Park Service. A section of the Network's website, which is still under development, will be map-based using an Internet Mapping Service (IMS) to provide access to spatially explicit data and allow users to explore Network data in a spatial context.
- Affected Staff – Data Manager, Science Writer, Program Managers, Network Coordinator.
- Purpose – Provide park staff and public access to all GLKN products and reports, describe the mission of the I&M Program, and provide current information about monitoring programs.
- Style – Primarily non-technical, but downloadable materials will be both technical and non-technical.

- Audience – All visitors to GLKN website, including park staff, partners and collaborators, and the public.
- Timeline – Updated regularly.

Beyond the Network's public website, potential websites to use in disseminating information include:

1. *Internal* (Intranet) sites:
   a. GLKN intranet
      www1.nrintra.nps.gov/im/units/glkn/index.cfm
   b. GLKN SharePoint
      http://imnetsharepoint/glkn/default.aspx
   c. InsideNPS
      http://inside.nps.gov/
   d. Midwest Region Natural Resources Science and Stewardship intranet
      http://midwest.nps.gov/office/natural/
   e. National I&M Program intranet
      www1.nrintra.nps.gov/im/
   f. NatureBib
      https://science1.nature.nps.gov/naturebib/nb/simple/clean
   g. NPSpecies
      https://science1.nature.nps.gov/npspecies/web/main/start

2. *External* (public) sites:
   a. Great Lakes Research and Education Center
      www.nps.gov/indu/naturescience/glrec.htm
   b. Individual GLKN Park web pages (via www.nps.gov)
   c. National I&M Program http://science.nature.nps.gov/im/index.cfm
   d. Park partner websites (via park staff) Examples: Isle Royale Institute, Friends groups, and Lake Superior National Parks Foundation.
   e. Great Lakes-Northern Forest Cooperative Ecosystem Studies Unit
      www.cesu.umn.edu

4. Purpose, Goals, and Objectives of the Great Lakes Network Outreach and Communications Effort

The goals, objectives, and strategies in this plan conform to the definitions and guidance in Asibey et al. (2008).

Purpose

To provide concise, meaningful communications in a timely manner to park natural resource managers, superintendents, and interpretive staff; our science partners, the public, and the scientific community outside of the National Park Service regarding the work and findings of the Great Lakes Inventory and Monitoring Program.

Goals

Goals are long-term in scope (5-10 years) and reflect the purpose of the Network's outreach and communications efforts.

Goals for this communication plan are:
1. Natural resource managers feel well-informed about the progress and current results of Network monitoring programs. They have enough information to share with park administrators, interpretive staff, and the public.
2. Superintendents feel well-informed about the progress and current results of the monitoring programs.
3. Interpretive staff are aware of the I&M program's work in their particular park, and they have some of the tools they need to share with the public information about and findings from Great Lakes Inventory and Monitoring programs.
4. The public has access to information about the Great Lakes Inventory and Monitoring Program and what we are learning from our monitoring programs.

Objectives

Objectives should be Specific, Measurable, Attainable, Result-focused, and Time-specific (SMART) statements that identify what the Great Lakes Network will do to meet our outreach and communication goals. Objectives should be completed in 1-2 years.

Goal 1. Natural resource managers are well-informed about the progress and current results of Network monitoring programs. They have enough information to share with park administrators, interpretive staff, and the public.

> Objective 1: Beginning in Spring 2008, we will publish and distribute a newsletter twice a year – spring and fall – to preview and summarize, respectively, that season's work.
> Objective 2: Program managers will complete an annual report that summarizes the field season and puts it into context with the past seasons. Annual reports may not be park-specific if work was done in more than one park that season, but the report will address each park's data individually.
> Objective 3: Superintendents and resource managers will receive annual, park-specific Resource Briefs for each monitoring program.

Goal 2. *Superintendents are well-informed about the progress and current results of the monitoring programs.*

Objective 1: We will provide superintendents with the newsletter, and data summary reports and Resource Briefs for each monitoring program in their park.

Goal 3. *Interpretive staff are aware of the I&M program's work in their particular park, and they have some of the tools they need to share with the public information about and findings from Great Lakes Inventory and Monitoring programs.*

Objective 1: We will provide park interpreters with one-page, park-specific resource briefs that summarize each GLKN monitoring program and its current findings.

Objective 2: We will provide brief articles about the monitoring programs and other topics of interest (as expressed by park staff) to park newspapers.

Goal 4. *The public has access to information about the Inventory and Monitoring Program and what we are finding.*

Objective 1: GLKN brochure is available to the public at park visitor centers.

Objective 2: GLKN resource briefs and site bulletin(s) are available to the public at park visitor centers.

Objective 3: GLKN resource briefs and site bulletin(s) are posted on GLKN and park web sites.

5. Evaluation

The usefulness and effectiveness of each communication tool and product will be evaluated after at least one year of use. Those media that prove to be ineffective for our purposes will be discontinued.

Interestingly, program evaluation has not been a standard component of the National Park Service's interpretive function. As noted in the current NPS interpretation and education action plan: "We have very little scientifically valid information about the direct outcomes and impact of interpretation and education programs" (NPSEC 2006: p. 6). As a result, the Great Lakes Network is both a learner and a participant in a new effort to "create a culture of evaluation" and ensure ongoing program improvement, effectiveness, and efficiency by making evaluation an integral part of program design and delivery (NPSEC 2006).

Tracking the Level of Impact

We need to know if we are providing the right products at the proper frequency to keep parks informed of what we are doing and what we are learning from our efforts. We also should evaluate if the information we are providing is what the parks need. Are the data and their subsequent interpretation appropriate for illuminating management issues and then guiding a management decision?

A communication program can be evaluated against three levels of potential impact (Table 1). Each level asks more specific questions about the communication products, the message contained in the products, the target audiences, and the impact the products had on the audiences.

Table 1. The three levels of potential impact for communication products and the questions to ask to evaluate those products (from Jacobson 1999).

Level 1	1. How much exposure did communications receive? 2. How many events, press releases, publications were produced? 3. Were the products likely to reach the target audience(s)?
Level 2	1. Did the target audience receive the message? 2. Did the target audience pay attention to the message? 3. Did the target audience understand the message? 4. Did the target audience retain the message? If so, in what form did the target audience retain the message?
Level 3	How did the communication products/message change the target audiences' opinions, attitudes, and/or behaviors?

The Great Lakes Network office already tracks the level of exposure our communications receive and the number of events, press releases, and publications produced (Level 1). We also qualitatively monitor if the target audiences receive our message, if they pay attention to it, and if they understand and retain it (Level 2). We do not evaluate the form in which the audiences retain the message (Level 2, question 4).

Evaluating Level 3 impacts has not been done by the Great Lakes Network, and it may not be feasible to do so until we begin publishing multi-year analyses of our monitoring data. Those reports will inform any management changes, and that is the true change in opinion, attitude, or behavior we are seeking. Changes in resource condition have been used to evaluate success of interpretive and other communications efforts (personal communication with Mike Whatley, National Park Service Natural Resource Program Center, Office of Education and Outreach). Still, there are some small management actions that have benefitted from the early data we have gathered and analyzed, even on a preliminary basis (e.g., disposal of hazardous waste at Outer Island lighthouse, Apostle Islands National Lakeshore, based on bioaccumulative contaminants information gathered from Bald Eagles there). Perhaps we can track published Superintendent's Orders or other management-related documents to measure our impact at this highest level.

Evaluation Techniques

Interviews

The Network Science Writer conducted introductory meetings and interviews with staff at each of the nine Network parks during the summer and fall of 2008. Visits focused on meeting resource managers and, when possible, superintendents and interpretive chiefs. The Science Writer also asked the resource managers to invite anyone else they thought might benefit from a discussion about communication between the park and the Network office. A summary of those meetings, and notes from each individual park meeting are provided in Appendix D.

The visits had a two-fold purpose. First, establish a face-to-face relationship between the Science Writer and the managers so that managers know who the "chief communicator" is, and so the Science Writer knew and understood the hierarchy of individuals in each park's resource management division.

Second, the meetings provided a forum for presenting the Science Writer's initial ideas for communicating with the parks and for collecting feedback on those ideas as well as suggestions for other communication avenues. Park staff were asked how they would like to see the information – should it be text only, or should the information be summarized in bullet points, photos, and graphs? How often did parks want to hear from the Network office? What sort of communication had the parks received from the Network office up to that point? Were their information needs were being met?

The meetings also provided a means for identifying the Science Writer's point of contact with each park. Some parks chose only one person (the resource manager), while others suggested sending information to a few principals (e.g., resource manager, superintendent, Chief of Interpretation), and each of them could then decide if they wanted to continue receiving information.

The Science Writer, during the course of regular visits to each Network park, will conduct informal, random interviews with park staff at visitor centers and within the resource management division to evaluate the availability and usefulness of I&M communication products. Secondary information to be gleaned from these interviews includes an evaluation of the point of contact's effectiveness in disseminating Network and park-specific monitoring information to park staff. Interview questions may include the following:

1. Do park staff know what the I&M program is?
2. Do park staff know they are part of the Great Lakes Inventory and Monitoring Network?
3. Do park staff know what monitoring programs are going on in their park?
4. Can the staff produce a Network publication, such as the brochure, a monitoring resource brief, or the Network newsletter?
5. Are Network publications (brochure, resource briefs, newsletters) available to the public in the park visitor centers?

Question 5 may also be answered by simply touring a park visitor center to see if and how Network publications are displayed.

Surveys

Each park will receive at least one survey by Email each year (Appendices B and C). The Email survey will be in two slightly different formats, one for natural resource management staff and the second for non-resource management staff. The survey's purpose will be to identify what Network publications the park staff are using and how effective those publications are in sharing information about resource monitoring both internally (for resource managers) and with the visiting public (for non-resource managers). They will also evaluate the communication structure within a park so we can determine if we are using the appropriate channels or if information is becoming "bottle-necked" somewhere. The survey will also solicit new communication product ideas and suggestions for modifications to existing items. Non-resource management surveys will be distributed through the "<PARK> All Employees" distribution lists.

Deadlines will be set for returning the surveys to the Science Writer, and phone calls will be made after that date has passed to follow up on unreturned surveys. Success in this effort will be defined by a minimum return rate of three surveys per park – one from a resource manager, one from an interpreter, and one from the Superintendent (or a designee) each year.

Thoughts for the Future – Challenges to Face

On a Personal Note

This plan is being completed after one full year of developing and distributing communications products and services to the Great Lakes Network parks has passed. The first year's work represents a composite of ideas I brought to the job, suggestions from Network staff, and things I heard from the staff of the Network parks during meetings with them. It has admittedly been a shotgun approach, but the sights on the gun were honed in to the best of our ability so that we did not waste time or money in setting up the lines of communication and putting out a few products people could see and consider. But there are still opportunities to be explored that are not expressed in these pages. For example, is there a way for me to work with parks when they re-visit their interpretive plans so that we can include information about Network monitoring programs? Or does that responsibility lie with the park resource management staff?

During our program review in March 2009, we repeatedly heard the suggestion to use "compelling stories" to communicate with the public about our work and why it's important. What are those stories? In his discussion of using stories to make current scientific conclusions relevant to the public, Whatley (1995) shares a quote from a former Chief of Interpretation at Rocky Mountain National Park: "By identifying and delivering the compelling stories, interpreters enable many different people to reexamine their own values and understand why these stories and resources are important." In this way, the listener/reader is motivated to action as "the message becomes theirs, not ours." Clearly there is power in viewing our work from this different perspective and then sharing what we see. This is no small challenge for scientists who are accustomed to a "just the facts" approach to their speaking and writing. But we will work on ways to gain this perspective and develop those stories. It can only result in helping to shape a bright future for our program and for our parks.

Whatley (1995) also discusses making natural resource data relevant to a park's purpose or mission by correlating it with past human activities. This is especially important in places like Grand Portage National Monument, and to some extent in the Mississippi National River and Recreation Area, "park areas set aside primarily for their cultural features." One (Grand Portage) is a relatively small, entirely cultural resource site that also happens to have some interesting natural resource issues. The other (Mississippi River) is a very urban park with almost no land base. Making the work of the Inventory and Monitoring Program relevant to these two parks has been an interesting exercise. Fortunately, both places are blessed with an enthusiastic staff who have a great interest in what we do. That part of the job is easy. The challenge as we go forward is how to make our findings relevant to what they deal with on a daily basis and what their visiting publics come to experience.

As a Network, we are struggling to clearly identify where the Network Science Writer's job overlaps and where it is distinct from the work of the Great Lakes Research and Education Center (GLREC). I think the Network's role is to provide the information (data) to the GLREC, who uses it to generate public education programs and products. The Network may produce some educational items, but ultimately our focus is on internal audiences rather than external audiences. The external audiences are the focus of the GLREC. Perhaps, too, the GLREC should develop information and education materials based on *all* of a park's research, inventory, and monitoring data, while the Network focuses solely on Network monitoring data. Some of these questions will hopefully be answered over the next few months as the GLREC completes its strategic plan and brings its steering committee on board. The Network and the Great Lakes-Northern Forest Cooperative Ecosystem Studies Unit will both have at-large seats at that table so that all three of us can do a better job of coordinating our efforts along with the parks.

Literature Cited

Asibey, E., T. Parras, and J. van Fleet. 2008. Are we there yet? A communications evaluation guide. Asibey Consulting, Brooklyn, NY, and The Communications Network, Naperville, IL. Online. (http://asibey.com/wp-content/uploads/2008/ 12/AreWeThereYet.pdf). Accessed 2 July 2009.

Beever, E., and S. Sanders. 2007. Chapter 7 – Analysis and reporting. Pages 105-116 *in* B. Route and J. Elias, editors. Long-term ecological monitoring plan: Great Lakes Inventory and Monitoring Network. Natural Resource Report NPS/GLKN/NRR—2007/001. National Park Service, Fort Collins, Colorado.

Fancy, S. 2004. An overview of vital signs monitoring and its central role in natural resource stewardship and performance management. National Park Service, Vital Signs Monitoring web site. http://science.nature.nps.gov/im/monitor/docs/.

Fancy, S. G. 2008. Connect the dots: A long-term strategic framework for connecting science and management through the park planning process. Unpublished paper, 7 July 2008 version.

Fancy, S. G., J. E. Gross, and S. L. Carter. 2009. Monitoring the condition of natural resources in U.S. National Parks. Environmental Monitoring and Assessment 151: 161-174.

Jacobson, S. K. 1999. Communication Skills for Conservation Professionals. Island Press, Washington, D.C.

National Park Service (NPS). 1999. Natural Resource Challenge: The National Park Service's action plan for preserving natural resources. U.S. Department of the Interior, National Park Service, Washington, D.C. (Online). http://www.nature.nps.gov/challenge/challengedoc/index.htm.

National Park Service Education Council (NPSEC). 2006. Interpretation and education renaissance action plan. National Park Service, Interpretation and Education Program, Washington, D.C.

Route, B. and J. Elias. 2007. Chapter 1 – Background information. Pages 5-32 *in* B. Route and J. Elias, editors. Long-term ecological monitoring plan: Great Lakes Inventory and Monitoring Network. Natural Resource Report NPS/GLKN/NRR—2007/001. National Park Service, Fort Collins, Colorado.

Sellars, R. W. 1997. Preserving Nature in the National Parks: A History. Yale University Press, New Haven, Connecticut.

Soukup, M. 2007. Integrating science and management: Becoming who we thought we were. George Wright Forum 24:26-29.

Whatley, M. E. 1995. Interpreting critical natural resource issues in Canadian and United States National Park Service areas. Natural Resources Report NPS/NRCACO/NRR-95/17. National Park Service, Natural Resources Publication Office, Denver, Colorado.

Appendix A. Example of a communications calendar for the Great Lakes Network.

January	15 – DRAFT annual summary reports ready for review Contact parks about providing articles for park newspaper 31 – DRAFT analysis and synthesis reports ready for review
February	
March	1 – FINAL annual summary reports sent to parks 15 – DRAFT Resource Briefs ready for review Western Great Lakes Research Conference Technical Committee meeting
April	1 – FINAL analysis/synthesis reports sent to parks 1 – FINAL Resource Briefs sent to parks 30 – Newsletter (season preview) to parks
May	Solicit parks for presentations to seasonal staff or all-staff training sessions
June	Seasonal Orientation/All-Staff training presentations (as requested) Park Lecture Series presentations (as requested)
July	Park Lecture Series presentations (as requested)
August	Park Lecture Series presentations (as requested)
September	
October	St. Croix Research Rendezvous 31 – Newsletter (season summary) to parks
November	FINAL annual administrative report and work plan sent to WASO
December	

Appendix B. Survey form for natural resource management staff to evaluate Network communication products.

Park _____

Date _____

Great Lakes I&M Network Communications Evaluation
(*Resource Management Staff*)

Please take a few minutes to answer these questions about the communication products distributed by the Great Lakes I&M Network office. These evaluations are being used to improve our communications and better serve your needs. Thank you.

1. Which of the following do you use, and how often?
   1 = I read them and file for future reference
   2 = I read them and I then circulate them to other park staff
   3 = I don't read them, but I circulate them to other park staff
   4 = I never use them, and I don't send them to anyone else

   Natural Resource Technical Reports (NRTR and NRR) _____

   Annual Reports from Network monitoring staff _____

   Fact Sheets for Network monitoring programs _____

   Network newsletter, *The Current* _____

   "News for Parks" emails _____

2. Of the publications you use or send to others, do you receive them often enough so that they are timely and useful? If not, when do you think would be a better time to send them out or how often should they come out?

3. Are there other types of communications products you think should be added? Any you think we should drop or significantly modify?

4. Do you have any other thoughts or suggestions about how we can better communicate our work and results with you and your park?

Appendix C. Survey form for non-resource management park staff to evaluate Network communication products.

Park _____

Date _____

Great Lakes I&M Network Communications Evaluation
(Non-Resource Management Staff)

Please take a few minutes to answer these questions about the communication products distributed by the Great Lakes I&M Network office. These evaluations are being used to improve our communications and better serve your needs. Thank you.

1. In what capacity do you work for the park?   Seasonal   Permanent   Volunteer

                                                        Protection /
   Administration   Maintenance   Interpretation   Law Enforcement

2. Are you aware of the monitoring programs being carried out by Network staff in your park?

                                   Yes   No

   If you answered "No" to question #2, you do not need to go any further. Please submit this evaluation as instructed.

3. How did you hear about the Network's monitoring programs in your park?

   | Email | Presentation by Network staff | Mentioned in a staff meeting | Publication sent around | Other _____ |

4. If you learned about Network monitoring in your park through a publication that was circulated, which publication was it? (Please check all that apply.)

           Natural Resource Technical Reports (NRTR and NRR) _____

           Annual Reports from Network monitoring staff _____

           Fact Sheets for Network monitoring programs _____

           Network newsletter, *The Current* _____

5. Of the publications you have seen, do you receive them often enough so that they are timely and useful? If not, when do you think would be a better time to send them out or how often should they come out?

6. Are there other types of communications products you think should be added? Any you think we should drop or significantly modify?

Please use the back of this paper to share any other thoughts or suggestions about how we can better communicate our work and results with you and your park.

Appendix D. A summary of feedback gathered during visits to Great Lakes Network parks in 2008

Overall Summary

Who should receive information?

SLBE	Susan Sanders (for Interp)
	Steve Yancho
	Dusty Schultz
VOYA	Steve Windels
	Tawnya Schoewe (for Interp)
MISS	Steve Johnson
	Nancy Duncan
PIRO	Bruce Leutscher
	Gregg Bruff (for Interp)
	Brenda St. Martin (for superintendent and for website)
ISRO	Mark Romanski
	Liz Valencia
APIS	Julie Van Stappen
	Myra Foster
	Neil Howk
GRPO	Dave Cooper
	Brandon Seitz
SACN	Kate Hanson
	Robin Maercklein
	Julie Galonska (for Interp)
INDU	Randy Knutson
	Brenda Waters
	Wendy Smith
	Joy Marburger
	Linda Lancaster (PIO)
	Kim Swift (park newspaper)

Want information to share at Seasonal Training
Steve Yancho, Steve Windels, Julie Galonska, Randy Knutson

Invited to give a presentation at Seasonal Training
ISRO

Interested in having Network staff prepare articles for park newspaper
SLBE, VOYA, PIRO, APIS

Suggestions:
1. Prepare menu of products and have people order what they want.
2. Include 1-2 "what can I do?" suggestions on fact sheets
3. So what? Why is this important?

   Tangible resource ⟶ *Intangible meaning* (what tool will connect the two?)
4. School curriculum program (Gregg Bruff recommended Dave Kronk at PIRO)
5. Feed information to Junior Ranger program
6. Emphasize connection to park and that GLKN is part of national program
7. Newsletter should emphasize the Big Picture

Individual Park Meeting Notes
The following notes indicate (in the "Who" line) the names of people I met whom I will likely be working with most in the future. The list does not include everyone that I met and talked to during the visit.

Sleeping Bear Dunes National Lakeshore
26 May 2008

Who: Susan Sanders, Lisa Myers (Chief of Interp), Marie Scott (Lead Interp), Steve Yancho

This meeting was preceded by a presentation to the SLBE staff about the Inventory and Monitoring Program and the Great Lakes Network. Those identified above are the "principals" who participated in a meeting after the presentation to discuss Network outreach and communication, but they are not all of the people who attended; others not named above were present and took part in the discussion.

Send information to Steve, Susan, and Dusty [Schultz, SLBE superintendent] individually. They can decide how to use and disseminate.

Send sampling schedules and names ahead of time so presentations can be set up (to the public or to park staff).

Prepare articles for Park newspaper. Steve thinking about developing RM newsletter.

Send Steve information to share at seasonal training (June).

Voyageurs National Park
23 July 2008

Who: Jim Hummel, Lee Grim, Mary Graves (Cultural Resources), Steve Windels, Cameron Trembath (Bio Tech), John Snyder, Catherine Crawford (Collections-Museum)

Send most information to Steve, and he will disseminate as needed.

Receiving briefing statements in April is best.

Tawnya Schoewe (Lead Interp) in charge of setting up Lecture Series.

Go through park for any press releases.

Have a poster at Seasonal Training.

A calendar that focuses on the parks, projects and the Network might be a good promotional item (similar to the invasives calendar put out by ??)

Newsletter – focus on big picture

Calendar of who, when, and where before field season.

Emphasize connection to park program. Also point out that there is a national I&M program, that GLKN is not the only Network.

Briefing statements – include text box with the take-home message, an excerpt. Examples in *Frontiers in Ecology and Environment* magazine ("In a Nutshell") and *Wildlifer*.

Feed information to Junior Ranger program?

Mississippi National River and Recreation Area
1 August 2008
Who: Steve Johnson, Nancy Duncan

MISS does formal education in schools. Have satellite interpretive centers in local and state parks.

Need web-friendly information (easy as possible)

Bird list coming from Minnesota Audubon. Citizen science bird monitoring protocol.

Corridor-specific information is hard to come by: Mammal list for MISS is actually from SACN. MISS is often confused with the Missouri River (especially in NPSpecies)

Steve would like to be central source of information for science/natural history of river, no matter who does the work.

Pictured Rocks National Lakeshore

6 August 2008

Who: Jim Northup (Superintendent), Lora Loope, Bruce Leutscher, Gregg Bruff (Interp)

Article about I&M program and the Vital Signs in the park newspaper would be helpful.

Climate change – what changes are we seeing now that relate to climate change?

Briefing statement about the I&M Network.

Would like box of 500 brochures. Digital format to put on website.

Feb/March – Fireside Chats

Posters that fit on public billboards (paired with brochure).

Newsletter – one/year=multi-page. >one/year=one-page. Send in Feb/March, which is down-time when people are most likely to read it.

Send PDF files.

Send to: Gregg, Bruce, Brenda St. Martin (website and superintendent's gate-keeper)

Gregg and Brenda handle public information duties.

Post slide shows online

Target publications/groups: Lake Superior Magazine, Sierra Club (Marquette), North Country Trail, Soo Naturalists

"Scout Ranger" program (cooperative NPS-BSA program)

School curriculum (Junior Ranger) program (see Dave Kronk)

Staff could wear mesh cruiser vests with arrowhead and GLKN logo on them?

Isle Royale National Park

21 August 2008

Who: Mark Romanski, Liz Valencia

Sending information by May/June is most useful.

I could come and give presentation at Seasonal Orientation (last week of May/beginning of June).

Briefing statements for staff; fact sheets for handing out to the public (with results – people always asking what research and monitoring is finding)

I can do press releases, but run by Liz (others?)

Jim Wiener for lecture in 2009?

Mark wants to do RM newsletter (Isle Royale Institute involved?)

Park staff don't get enough information about resource management work (research, monitoring), but there is a GREAT demand for it, great interest.

Send information to Liz directly (in addition to Mark *et al.*)

Apostle Islands National Lakeshore
4 September 2008
Who: Neil Howk, Myra Foster

I spoke with Resource Management staff Julie Van Stappen and Peggy Burkman earlier in the summer of 2008, and I met with Superintendent Bob Krumenaker in March 2009.

Briefing statement – change name. "Briefing statement" has a particular meaning in NPS.

So what? Why is this important?

Interpretive Development Program (www.nps.gov/idp/interp) – Standards for Interpretive Media

Tangible resource – Intangible meaning (what tool will connect the two?)

University of Indiana – Fundamentals of Interpretation. Online courses (Epply Institute: www.parktraining.org)

Possible venues:
1. Lunch presentation in winter (see Jennifer Boulley)
2. Summer Lecture Series (see Betsy Bartelt)
3. Mid-summer gathering on Stockton – campfire program, special research event
4. Supervisor's meeting
5. All-Park meeting

Park newspaper put together in March/April (Neil). Request for contributions goes out ca. February.

Damon Panek and Greg Zeman maintain the website. Something on NR page? – Why does this matter?

See "Inside Yellowstone" – video files on website. Also being done at Glacier.

Grand Portage National Monument
23 September 2008
Who: Dave Cooper, Brandon Seitz

Park website is best place for materials.

Grand Marais for evening programs.

Writing newspaper article is good idea.

Send everything to Dave and copy Brandon.

St. Croix National Scenic Riverway
22 October 2008
Who: Kate Hanson, Robin Maercklein, Becky Haass, Byron Karns, Jill Medland, Julie Galonska (Interp), Jean Schaeppi (Cultural Resources and web site person)

1-2 suggestions ("what can I do?") on fact sheets would be good.

Video to show at Seasonal Training?

Send print copies, not PDFs (except to post on website)

Send I&M brochure

"Conversations in the Valley" hosted by St. Croix Community Foundation (Jill Shannon) held in Stillwater each Tuesday from September to May. No public lecture series at VC during the summer.

Interpretive handouts (eagles). Dragonfly and mussel brochures are the most popular here. Used for state park and high school programs (connect with teachers). Staff do school programs.

Send information to Kate, Robin, and Julie.

Park-specific monitoring could be shown on back of site bulletin.

Communications Plan being developed for SACN – draft due by Spring 2009.

Indiana Dunes National Lakeshore

18 November 2008

Who: Randy Knutson, Brenda Waters, Wendy Smith, Joy Marburger, Bob Daum, Lynda Lancaster (Public Information Officer), Bruce Rowe (Supervisory Park Ranger/Interp), Judy Collins (Historical Architect), Kim Swift (Education Specialist)

Janet Ambrose is Chief of Interp (not available today).

Offer a menu of products people can order from.

Tying in our work with what others (e.g., USGS) are doing in the park would be more comprehensive.

Kim Swift puts Park Newspaper together.

Can we do workshops with researchers?

Park does online podcasts (virtual visit) similar to "Inside Yellowstone." Have the expertise and the equipment in-house to do these.

NPS 999/100544, October 2009